Last Easter

Bryony Lavery's plays include *Frozen* (TMA Best Play, Eileen Anderson Central Television Award and four Tony nominations), *Stockholm* (Wolff-Whiting Award, Best Play, 2008), *Beautiful Burnout* (Fringe First), *A Wedding Story*, *Last Easter*, *Her Aching Heart* (Pink Paper Play of the Year, 1992), *Dirt*, *The Believers* and *Queen Coal*. Her stage adaptations include *101 Dalmations*, *A Christmas Carol*, *Precious Bane*, *The Wicked Lady*, *Treasure Island* (National Theatre), *Brighton Rock* and *The Lovely Bones*. She is a member of the Royal Society of Literature, an honorary Doctor of Arts at De Montford University and an associate artist of Birmingham Repertory Theatre.

BRYONY LAVERY

Last Easter

faber

First published in 2007 by Faber & Faber Limited
74–77 Great Russell Street London WC1B 3DA

Typeset by Country Setting, Kingsdown, Kent CT14 3AU
Printed and bound in the UK by CPI Group (Ltd), Croydon CR0 4YY

Applications for performance, including readings and excerpts, by amateurs in the English
language throughout the world should be addressed to the Performing Rights Manager,
Nick Hern Books, The Glasshouse, 49a Goldhawk Road, London W12 8QP,
tel +44 (0)20 8749 4953, *email* rights@nickhernbooks.co.uk, except as follows:

Australia: ORiGiN Theatrical, Level 1, 213 Clarence Street, Sydney NSW 2000,
tel +61 (2) 8514 5201, *email* enquiries@originmusic.com.au,
web www.origintheatrical.com.au

New Zealand: Play Bureau, PO Box 9013, St Clair, Dunedin 9047, *tel* (3) 455 9959,
email info@playbureau.com

United States of America and Canada: United Agents, see details below.

Applications for performance by professionals in any medium and in any language
throughout the world should be addressed to United Agents, 12–26 Lexington Street,
London W1F 0LE, *tel* +44 (0)20 3214 0800, *fax* +44 (0)20 3214 0801,
email info@unitedagents.co.uk

No performance of any kind may be given unless a licence has been obtained. Applications
should be made before rehearsals begin. Publication of this play does not necessarily indicate
its availability for amateur performance.

A CIP record for this book is available from the British Library

978-0-571-23915-3

4 6 8 10 9 7 5 3

Acknowledgements

The newspaper article June refers to is by James Meek, from *The Guardian*, Wednesday, 10 November 1999. The (fictional) documentary details were from the same article. I also read Elizabeth Summerfield's article 'Why I Killed My Mother'(*Guardian*, 6 December 2000) for the effects of morphine on a terminal cancer patient; Natasha Walter's 'What Matters is Relief from Suffering' (*The Independent*, 18 June 2001) and Alison Kingsley's 'I Watched My Mother Kill Herself' (*Daily Mirror*, 14 April 2001).

I thank the wonderful jokers who told me all the jokes, including the late great Bob Monkhouse, Bill Clinton and the *Daily Mirror*'s 'Greet the New Year with a Smile and Enjoy Our Great Joke Bonanza', 31 December 2001.

Everybody concerned for the yearly reruns of *Easter Parade* . . .

The *Genius of Rome* exhibition at the Royal Academy for bringing 'The Taking of Christ' to my own city.

Also, Margot Gordon for my stay in her *gite* in Ponsan San Soubiron; Fiona Cunningham-Reid for thinking it would be 'really interesting to have a day out in Lourdes'; and Suzanne Bertish for the body-altering experience of her *linguini a la Genovese*.

And particularly to Su Elliott, Pippa Sparkes and Buffy Davies for their humour and grace in caring for their friend Sally Greenwood, who departed this life far too early, but still swearing.

Bryony Lavery

The world premiere of **Last Easter** was presented by MCC Theatre at the Lucille Lortel Theatre, New York, on 7 October 2004. The cast was as follows:

Gash Jeffrey Carlson
June Veanne Cox
Howie Jeffrey Scott Green
Leah Clea Lewis
Joy Florencia V. Lozano

Director Doug Hughes
Scenic Designer Hugh Landwehr
Costume Designer Catherine Zuber
Lighting Designer Clifton Taylor
Original Music and Sound Designer Fabian Obispo

Last Easter premiered in the UK at The Door, Birmingham Repertory Theatre, on 18 October 2007. The cast was as follows:

June Janet Dibley
Gash Peter Polycarpou
Leah Caroline Faber
Joy Christine Kavanagh

Director Douglas Hodge
Designer Soutra Gilmour
Lighting Designer Ben Ormerod
Stage Manager Liz Vass

Last Easter was revived at the Orange Tree Theatre, Richmond, on 7 July 2021. The cast was as follows:

June Naana Agyei-Ampadu
Gash Peter Caulfield
Leah Jodie Jacobs
Joy Ellie Piercy

Director Tinuke Craig
Designer Hannah Wolfe
Lighting Designer Elliot Griggs
Sound Director Beth Duke
Casting Consultant for 2021 Production
    Christopher Worrall CDG
Casting Consultant for Original 2020 Production
    Anne McNulty CDG
Casting Coordinator Sarah Murray

Characters

in order of appearance

Gash
a singer/female impersonator

Leah
a prop-maker

June
a lighting designer

Joy
an actor

The action takes place over two recent Easters

The lighting is wonderful beyond belief

The odd line lengths
weird   spacing
and plethora of exclamation marks
and question marks in the text
are the author's attempt to convey
the frenetic nature of these characters
in their situation!!!

/ in the text indicates one character
talking over another

Gash is playing 'Easter Parade' on the piano. He plays
the end of phrases deliberately out of tune. He pretends
to be unaware of this.
   June lights him and Leah.

Gash
   Easter. Last.
   We're sitting around, me and Leah . . .

   He's not physically working. Leah is. She's making
   something complicated.

   (*For Leah.*) This woman.
   She's making a cake.
   Huge cake.
   And she falls into the bowl
   of cake mix.
   Dies.

Leah
   How come?

Gash
   She's pulled under
   by a very strong currant.

   He plays 'boo-boom!' on the piano.

   Leah smiles a little.

   (*To us.*) We're trying to
   cheer each other up
   because
   okay

June   this friend
the bitch
June's had breast cancer . . .

Lights on June.

June
I'm sitting in my kitchen
here   a brown jug of
red tulips
they've opened and
they're like . . .

*A mime of 'They're all open, curvy, wavy stems gone
mad . . .'*

Very irritated with them . . .

'Yoohoo . . . We're Alive!'

I'm doing the *Guardian*
crossword.
Cryptic. I'm quite bright.

Radio Four fan.

There. Open door.
My minuscule
but beautiful garden.

Lights sideways from a garden . . .

Early March. Some cold
air . . . just
reaching me.
Just here. Cigarette.
Yeah . . . I know!
But . . . f-f-f-f- (*fuck it*).

Leah
It's her Extreme Sport.

June
    Also
    there's an excuse

    and
    there's absolutely no
    reason for it

    I'm
    completely happy.
    It's important you remember
    this.
    The happiness is something
    to do
    with . . . the air the sun the
    everything . . .

    She looks at the lights . . .

    the light
    particularly the light

    maybe, even, controversially,
    the cigarette.

    The phone goes.

    I pick it up.

    Hello?
    yes
    yes it is
    yes I am
    yes
    no, I don't need to come
    and see you
    just tell me
    yes
    no we did suspect that
    yes

is it
can we?
no
I'm okay
no . . . I'm okay
I sort of . . . yes
yes
yes
yes
no
don't worry
no
I'm alright
I was just about to go
out . . .
but I might . . .
I'm fine
no, I'm fine
really
I'll make an appointment.
Er . . . thank you.
Yes goodbye
bye

bye.

Phone down . . .

'Thank you'??????

Lights on Leah and Gash.

Gash *(to Leah)*
This man.
Goes to the doctor's.
Both his ears are stuffed
with scrambled egg.
He's got a rasher of bacon
wedged up each nostril.

Doctor says . . .
'What seems to be the
matter?'
and the man says
'I feel really awful . . .'
and the doctor says . . .
'Well . . . it's obvious . . .
you're not eating
properly . . .!'

Gash and Leah laugh, then . . .

(*To us.*) June's not eating
properly . . .
Not coming about.
Not snapping out of it . . .
It's soo irritating . . .

June
It's secondary cancer.
Cancer is 'a neoplasm',
apparently . . .
which has 'the ability to
leave home
and travel somewhere else'.
Sort of   Disease-Package-Tourist
So. Breast

She traces somehow the cancer route as she sings 'The Birdie Song' . . .

*diddlediddlediddle dit
diddlediddle dit diddle diddle diddle dit dit dit dit
dit . . . to*

Liver.

Look at these tulips.
Only three days
and they're starting

to . . . (*droop*).
Such a short life,
tulips . . .
Oh, shut up!

Gash (*to Leah*)
This man.
Goes to the doctor's . . .
He says . . .
'Doctor, doctor . . .
I keep thinking I'm a pair
of curtains . . .'
The doctor says . . .

Both
'Oh . . . pull yourself
together . . .'

Both smile wanly . . .

Gash
This man goes to the
doctor's,
he says,
'Doctor, doctor . . . I keep
thinking
I'm a pack of cards . . .'
The doctor says . . .

Both
'Sit down . . . I'll deal with
you in
a minute . . .'

Gash (*to us*)
We're not loving
doctors at this
particular moment in time.

June
   No.
   No.
   No!!!!!

Gash (*to Leah*)
   Two nurses.
   The Ugly Nurse says,
   'I was giving that patient a
   bath
   . . . and I look . . . see
   he's got "Ludo" tattooed on
   his willy!'
   The Pretty Nurse says, 'It's
   not "Ludo"
   It's "Llandudno".

   Gash and Leah laugh.

Leah (*to us*)
   We like nurses.

Gash
   Particularly in uniform.

   Leah nods.

June
   Yes. We do.
   But.
   Suddenly
   the happiness has
   vaporised
   the tulips the newspaper
   the kitchen
   not enough
   so just enough energy in the
   old   organism
   to Get Out!

She's at . . .

Go to this Exhibition.
Caravaggio.
I told you about it

Gash and Leah's heads alter to listen.
June is sitting, really, really looking at . . .

With the picture.

'The Taking of Christ' by Caravaggio arrives before
her.

It's
the most beautiful thing
I have ever seen.
Caravaggio
for Me
he is   It!
The Big Cheese!
Le Grand Fromage!

Gash (*or more linguistically appropriate*)
  Il Formaggio
  Grande . . . !

June looks hard, hard. It is better than crying.

June
  This   is
  miraculous!

  It's   what
  One-thirty by . . . one-sixty?
  centimetres
  It's one-thirty by one-sixty
  centimetres
  of pure pure genius.

  We're in the presence
  of greatness.

Leah
> Pay attention, Gash,
> We're in the presence of
> greatness.

Leah and Gash pay attention.

June
> It's called
> 'The Taking of Christ'.

Gash
> Oooh, he's taken me . . .

June
> Judas has just kissed Jesus
> their faces are   the
> heartbreak
> the pain
> yellowish light . . . just left
> of Jesus . . .
> a disciple . . .

June duplicates the disciple's outstretched hand and open, protesting mouth.

> a soldier armour
> orange doublet-hose-
> type thing has just . . .

Her arm reaches out.

> touched Jesus's sleeve . . . and
> there's
> a light . . . his fingers
> along the metal . . .
> of his armoured
> arm . . . helmet . . .
> and . . . down the . . .

Her other hand traces this.

breastplate . . . and onto this
orange . . . full
of buttock . . .

Gash

Buttock! Paying attention!!!

June

and . . . oh, God!!! . . . the
hands!
Christ's
hands! . . . They're . . .

With her hands, June shows them, fingers intermeshed.

out of oil paint and
rectangle of
and

Touches her brain.

this and

Touches her eyes.

these

Looks at her hands.

these

Back to the painting.

the light's coming from . . .
this lantern here . . .
a man's holding it . . . here . . .

*She shows us. Then looks slightly off to the left, where
the sign reads:*

'Caravaggio's nocturnal vision
includes two different light
sources,
an internal one from the

lantern and
an external one from the
unseen moon . . .'

She estimates.

moon
here

Reads again.

'The man holding the lantern's
a
self-portrait of
Caravaggio . . .'

Gash
Bit of a man for the models,
Caravaggio!
Ay, soldier?
Ay, Jesus?

June
Lantern
here.

Reads again.

'Perhaps, since Caravaggio
portrayed
himself illuminating the
subject with a
lantern, he wished the
viewer to accept
his decision as an eye-
witness account . . .
and thus underscore both the
truth and the realism
of the scene . . .'

He's about   dark and light.

Gash

Who isn't?

June

Light

light

light.

Leah/Gash

Yes, June.
Light!

Gash

June is a lighting designer.

Leah

We *love* June . . .

Gash

But . . . she's slightly 'Me!
Sun. You . . .

Leah

Dim bulbs.'

Gash

And . . . *plus* . . .

June

Breast cancer is casting a
Long Shadow.
I had this breast removed.
A selection of lymph nodes.
Don't go there.
All this isn't a Big Tragedy
about that.

Gash/Leah

Yeah, right!

Gash
But At The Time Of Which We
Speak . . .
She's not firing on all
cylinders.

Leah
But   she's our
friend . . .

Gash
Oh come on . . .!
You kind of have to
sacrifice
the notion of friend as
interesting, complex, multi-
layered
smoking drinking shagging
chum for . . .
this sick tired bald twig
thing
in a polystyrene wig
you can't even laugh at . . .

June
you *are* allowed to laugh at . . .

Leah
She said you could laugh at
it!

June
Thank you!

Gash
Permission!
How's that fun???

Leah
And it is real hair,
actually . . .

June
just not *my* real hair . . .

Gash
Oh well, excuse me! . . . This
sick tired
bald twig thing in a wig of
real hair

June
. . . you can't even laugh at!

Leah waits.

Gash
Well, you know how shallow I
am.

Leah/June
Mmm!

June
Actually . . . then . . . I did
look . . . (*awful*).

Leah waits.

Gash
It makes her look like that
monkey in
Planet of the Apes.

Leah
Remake?
Helena Bonham Carter. (*Which isn't that bad.*)

Gash
Original

Leah
Kim Hunter. (*Which is.*)

Leah waits.

Gash
And when she doesn't wear it . . .
she looks like that house
dwarf thing in Harry Potter.

June/Gash
Dobby . . .

Gash
See?

Leah waits.

And she won't Talk about
it!!!

Leah waits.

Oh . . . Mary!

Gash burst into tears. Leah pats his head.

No!
don't!
oh!
Mary-Louise!
mascara!

Gash storms out.

Leah
Gash . . . He's very
emotional . . . for a Brit.

June
What'll happen now . . .
after he's repaired his
maquillage . . .

Leah

he'll go outside

Leah runs to watch, taking her work with her.

June

and   he'll stand
watching the ebb and flow of
people passing by . . .
and
there'll be someone who'll
meet his eye
man
boy
soldier
that look   you and I
would miss it.

Leah

I've been dancing *cheek to
cheek* with Gash
and I've missed it!

June

and
and this is the miracle . . .
there is always someone . . .
when he needs them . . .

Leah

and the two of them will nip
up an alley

June

and
zip
buttons
willies
rub blow

Ludo . . .

Llandudno.

Leah calls.

Leah
A painter and decorator!
Tracksuit bottoms . . .
Paint! Plaster!
I mean . . .
I'd look . . . think . . . he's a
Painter and decorator . . .
I wonder if he could give me
an
estimate for the hallway
Gash looks . . . for no
charge . . .
gets him to brighten
up his rear extension!

Gash returns.

Gash
Sorry.
Just popped out for . . .

Leah/June
a paint job . . .

Gash
It's beautiful out there
like summer
sun's actually burning my
face . . .

Leah
and your ass.

Gash
Shut your face.

Leah
Shut your ass.

June
But the miracle here is . . .

Gash
He was *French*.

June
Monsieur Le Decorateur.

Leah
You had a *conversation* with
him?

June
This is a relationship!

Gash
He was like '*Merrrrde!*'
when he came.

Leah
Not '*Ouf! Nous y voila!*'?

. . . that's what it said in
our French book . . .

Gash
When you come?

Leah
No! Well . . . When you arrive!
On French soil!
You say
'*Ouf! Nous y voila!*'

June
Look how the light picks out
the beautiful painting of
Christ

the departure of happiness
the discussion of French
idioms
the spring sun warming
Gash's face

Leah
and buttocks

June
God, apparently, is in the
details

Gash
Merde!
(*As lover.*) *Je t'aime France!*

Leah
Moi aussi!

June
This is the moment . . .

Leah
You know what?
We should take June off on a
holiday!
France!

June
All the great inventions . . .
the filament in an electric
light . . .
Pythagoras theory
$E=mc^2$
in all the great moments
in all the apparent mistakes . . .
God's there . . .

Gash
France! I've got a friend's
got a villa!

June
Gash always has a friend
who's got a . . .

Gash
Creepy Carl!

June
God's there . . .
Creeping . . .

Leah
Change of scenery for her

Gash
change of scenery for *us*.

June
Establishing the *mise-en-scène*.
His wonders to perform.

Leah
Perk her up

Gash
perk *us* up.

June
And they look, the two of
them, on the map . . .

Leah
Hey . . . Creepy Carl's villa's
Near somewhere called
'Condom'

Leah/Gash find this very funny and little bit mystical.

28

Gash

It's actually quite near
Lourdes!

June

Gash is a Catholic.

Leah

Lourdes?
Daughter of Madonna?

June

Leah is American.

Gash

Lourdes!
Miracle Capital of the
Western World!
The Holy Grotto!
St Bernadette!
Holy Water!
We could take her to
Lourdes!

June

Lourdes . . . Home of Miraculous
Recoveries . . .

Gash

Push her in the Holy Pool . . .

Pray for . . .

Leah/Gash

A miracle.

Gash

It could happen!

June

I'm June.

Look at me.
I'm the miracle.

Leah
I don't think we should Big
Up the Lourdes
Thing . . .

Gash
God, no! We shouldn't even
tell her!
She's so 'Religion??? . . . I
Don't Think So!'

June
The only thing I find
religion's got going
for it is The Lighting . . .

Gash
We'll keep it very low
key . . .
Be driving around . . . you'll
have the map . . .
say . . .

Leah (*bravura but bad acting*)
Hey,
look
 . . . we're quite near Lourdes!
Might be interesting . . . hey,
June?

A better line would be:

For me   as an
American

An even better line would be:

For me   as a Jew

30

Or for you, June, from a
purely anti-religious
standpoint.
Why don't we / just . . .

Gash
/ Something like that.

June
So the plan is . . .
My dear friends are going to take me to Lourdes
And   I'm going to be miraculously cured
Of secondary cancer
A disease from which   no one   recovers . . .
Cured by a phenomenon I deeply doubt
Celebrated by a Faith I don't believe in
Without my knowing it . . .

Gash
We'll ask St Bernadette to
at least
have her hair grow back . . .

June
Well . . . nothing else is
working . . .
The Bristol Diet
All Western medicine
All alternative medicine
Positive thinking . . .

Leah
We go round . . .

Gash
Froggies! Villa! Sun!

Leah
She's . . .

June
  France? Sure Yes Why
  not?
  Whereabouts?

Gash (*to Leah*)
  Map. Keep your
  thumb over 'Lourdes'.

They show June, Leah doing Lourdes-covering.

June (*to us*)
  Gives them a
  project. Bless.
  And

  hey   *pour moi*?

  last bloody holiday . . .

Gash
  Diaries.

They all get out their diaries, Gash and Leah following speeches at the same time. June looks at her diary while . . .

I've got two shows Brighton
twenty-first and twenty-
second . . .
Leg-waxing with Leon on the
eighteenth . . .
but I can change that get
that earlier . . .
it's Twink's party on the
nineteenth
but I'd only get *unnecessary*
at that so . . .
what about the week of the
twenty-fifth?

Leah

    Well . . . I can't miss the
    fourteenth because
    I'm propping *Absurd Person*
    Singular
    . . . eighteenth West
    Yorkshire's talking
    to me about *The Dream* but
    it's Guess Who?
    and after the Scottish Play
    I'm thinking forget it . . .
    I should go back across the
    Pond, see the Aged Parents
    but I could hold on that and
    go for
    their wedding anniversary
    thirty-two
    years never a cross word . . .

June

    The sixteenth? No.
    Therapy. The
    nineteenth?
    No . . . consultant.
    After that . . . only thing I've
    got is . . .
    cancer . . .
    . . . and I can bring that
    with me . . .

Gash

    Creepy Carl wants an
    indecent
    stash of loot to cover
    electricity gas Fabergé
    fucking eggs . . .

Leah
How much?

Gash
And I shagged him to get the
price down . . .

June
Nobody's personal vehicle's
up to it.

Gash
We're going to have to go
Rental . . .

June
Can we go for comfort not
colour this time?

Leah
You know what . . .
there's space for one
more . . .
We could cut Financial
Outlay by twenty-five per cent . . .

This is well worth applying brain power to . . .

Gash
Pretty Barry.

Leah
No!

June/Gash
Sorry! Forgot!!!

June
Tristram?

Leah
Too mean. Chris?

Gash
Not mean enough.

They think.

Leah
Jessica?

June
The Penetrating Body Odour
Thing.

Leah
Perfect Pamela?

Gash
The Vegan Thing.

Leah
Sandy Scrivener?

All
The Relentless Cheeriness.

Gash
Must be *somebody* . . .

Finally . . .

All Three
Joy . . . ????

As June lights . . .

Leah
Joy.

Joy somewhere, very very drunk.

Joy
Shall we have another?

Shall we have another bottle?

Shall we?

Howie?
How . . . ward???

Les have another bottle

Les

Hey! Hey! Can
we . . . yes . . . please
can we have another . . . what
was that
we were . . . a *Côtes du
Rhône* . . . that was
delicious, was it . . . ?
we'd like another of . . . is it
this . . . it's a . . .
it was red

might as well be drunk as the
way
we are, Darling . . . !

Don' go!
Jussst one more . . .
Don't . . .
Howie!!!!

Fuck you
Fuck you
Fuck it!

Lights down on Joy.

Leah/Gash
Perfect!

Gash
And we know she won't be
bringing Howie . . .

Leah
Behave!

June
And this is how
that Easter
with my awful wig of real
hair
looking like Kim Hunter

Leah
in the *original Planet of the
Apes*

June
I'm
in a French
Hire Car
somewhere
in South-West France . . .

*Leah, Gash and June singing . . . Joy, in dark glasses,
enormous hangover in a somehow-created car.*

Leah
Ouf! Nous y voila!
Drive on *The Right!*

Gash (*sings*)
'Never saw you look
quite so pretty before . . .'

Leah (*sings back*)
'Never saw you
dress
quite so handsome what's more . . .'

Both (*singing harmony*)
'I could
hardly wait

to keep our date
this lovely Easter morning
and my heart beat fast
as I came through
the door . . .
for . . .'

Joy (*hopefully*)
No loud singing . . .

All Three (*loud*)
'In your Easter bonnet
with all the frills upon it
you'll be the finest fellow
at the Easter Parade . . .'

Joy
No loud singing!

Enough singing, thank you!

No singing in the Rental Car!

Ooooh!

Oooooh!

The pain . . .!

June!
I need to . . . (*lean against her*)
and I need . . . (*cigarette*)

Oh God . . . I'm really
suffering, guys . . .

Leah
No smoking in The Hire Car!
We agreed!

Joy
This is a Terminal Hangover,
darling!

Last Wish Of A Dying Woman.
I'm dying here!

Leah
Joy! Shhh!

Joy (*stage whisper*)
Oh, what have
I said?
I didn't mention Lourdes!!!

Leah (*mouths*)
Dying. Terminal.
Shhh.

Joy
I'm not supposed to say? Not
mention the
D word or the T word or the
C word? Fuck Off!
I'm Terminal . . . not . . .
Oh fuck! fuck them
fuck pussyfooting around
fuck France fuck everything
fuck you!

Gash (*singing*)
'On the avenue
Fifth Avenue . . .
the photographers
will snap us
and you'll find that you're
in the rotogravure . . .'

Etc as . . .

Leah
Joy, will you just . . . (*zip it*)
alright? alright . . . ?

Gash (*big finish*)
　'Oh, I could write
　a sonnet . . .'

Joy
　Actually, darling, no more
　singing or talking
　no more fucking talking about
　it I need a drink
　We need a drink
　Yes! We do!

Gash
　You know . . . Garland, Me? One
　Soul!
　When she died . . .
　her spirit passed from her
　to me!

Joy
　Are you allowed to drink,
　Junie?
　No? Yes . . . Yes Yes!
　Of course you are this is a
　holiday I mean this is France
　should we have a little
　Côtes du Rhône or something?

June
　It's　　great to see
　you, Joy.

Joy
　Demonstrate your pleasure,
　Juney.
　Take me to some *Côtes du Rhône*.

Leah
　And

Lights.

French Lunch. Shellfish.
Baguette.

Gash (*it's a miracle*)
Loaves and
Fishes!

Leah
Shellfish . . . I shouldn't . . . (*But she does.*)
Oh well . . .

Gash (*it's a miracle*)
The Conversion
of the Jews!

Joy
Let's get . . . *une autre bouteille
de c'et* . . .
Monsieur! . . .
Not *everybody's* driving,
Leah . . . !!!

Leah
Dessert is some ceramic-
looking coulis. Drizzled over
Myrtle crêpes! Myrtle! Crêpes!

June
Then Gash, beautiful acting
job, says . . .

Gash
Hey, Intrepid Travellers . . .
we're quite near . . . Lourdes!

June
And Leah has a line . . .

Leah (*not as good acting*)
　　Lourdes!
　　Hey . . . Lourdes!
　　As an Americ . . . as a Jew I've
　　never been to Lourdes!
　　That might be interesting for
　　me
　　in a purely investigative sort
　　of way . . .
　　Why don't we go to Lourdes?

Gash
　　Might be Fun!

Joy
　　Why don't we finish with
　　a real drink?

　　Monsieur . . . ? *Cognac, s'il
　　vous . . .*

　　She catches the others' eyes.

　　No. Lourdes!!! Good Idea!!!
　　What do you think . . . June?

　　All but June breathe in . . .

June
　　And I say 'Lourdes?'

　　and I get a flash of   healing
　　hands

　　here   and here
　　so I go   with
　　majestical calm
　　'Lourdes? Great! Why not?'
　　All the acting is impeccable . . .

42

Others
    Great!

June
    We take the road to Lourdes . . .

    Other three breathe out . . .

Leah (*reading from guidebook*)
    'The
    visionary of Lourdes
    and later nun, Bernadette, was
    the daughter
    of François Soubirous, a miller,
    and
    was the oldest of six children,
    who,
    for various reasons, lived in
    acute
    poverty . . .'

Gash
    Acute poverty. It's Me!

Leah (*reading*)
    'She was an undersized,
    ailing
    child who suffered from
    asthma . . .'

Gash
    Undersized. Ailing. It's me!
    I could do a St Bernadette show!
    With Garland songs!

Leah (*reading*)
    'Her intellectual
    equipment
    was simple, and some witnesses
    thought her stupid . . .'

Joy
    Simple. Stupid. It is You.

Leah (*reading*)
    'But her veracity,
    courage
    and complete disinterestedness
    are beyond dispute.'

Gash
    It is Me!

Leah (*reading*)
    'At the age of
    fourteen,
    in 1858
    she experienced in the space of
    six months a series of eighteen
    visions of the Blessed Virgin
    Mary . . .'

Gash
    Oh, it's the Virgin Mary
    Oh, it's the Virgin Mary
    Oh, it's the Virgin Mary
    Oh it's the . . .

    He continues until:

Others
    Shut Up, St Bernadette!

Leah
    You'd be too stupid and
    undernourished
    to count to eighteen!

June (*to Gash*)
    Be real.

Gash (*as Bernadette, a good acting job right there in the car . . .*)
. . . Was Our Lady
Was Our Lady
Was Our Lady
in our field!
there   right there right
just there!
I don' ask no
I don' ask no
becas   I don'
she poin's the rock.
'Drink. This water yere.'
I does
then
'Make a church yere. You.'
And our Lady says . . .

June
Joy. You.
Adventurous casting.

Joy (*cooey, Our Lady voice*)
'Make a church here.
You!
Little peasant creature . . .'

Gash
And discover . . . Tourism?

Joy
'Yes, my child.
Get on with it while I have a
little snooze
on the left hand of God . . .'
(*As herself.*) Fucking apparitions.

Leah
Joy! Language! Respect!

45

Joy
Fucking 'Here We Are Again!' Apparitions!!

June
We approach Lourdes . . .

They put on beautiful music . . . they all want a miracle, but it's each person's secret . . .

Gash
I'm feeling full of tears don't
know why . . .

Leah
Steep mountains
slightly shrouded in mist . . .

I'm feeling very Jewish! . . .

Mountains . . . mist appear . . .

Gash
We're like Brad and Janet in
The Rocky Horror Show . . .
driving towards our doom . . .

June
We descend . . .

Leah
Lourdes Miracle Centre of Europe
is packed

Joy
Ungh!

Leah
with your gentiles . . .!

June
thronged with people

Leah
shops selling Catholic
tchatkes . . .

Gash
I buy this table lamp of
St Bernadette
standing in the pool . . . rocks
around her
feet . . . plug her in . . . her halo
lights up . . .
and all her robes glow in the
dark . . .!
I'll show you it later . . .

June
It's in a valley
and a rushing sparkling lively
shallow
river runs through it . . .

Rushing water somewhere . . .

Leah
There's a statue of   some
Christian . . .

She shows us . . .

June
with a dove of peace sticking out
of
its head.

Gash
I'm raining tears.

Leah
You okay?

Gash
　All my dead people have come
　with me . . . my mother, Terry,
　Jules . . . Pedro . . .
　Six-Pack Stephen . . .
　Camp David . . .

　Joy and Leah pat him . . .

Joy
　I'm so glad fucking Howie's not
　here!

　Gash and Leah pat her.

　Stop!
　Stop!
　Stop!

June
　We're in the thick of it . . .

Leah
　By the river
　close to the Grotto

Gash
　I notice
　everywhere
　these loudspeakers (*Up.*)
　and I'm thinking
　'What are those for?' when . . .

　Loud, amplified 'Shhhhh' is heard . . .

All (*except June, whispered*)
　They're for 'shhh'ing
　you.

Leah　(*thoroughly shushed*)
　It works.

Everybody goes quiet and
respectful . . .

Gash
Except the Italians! Who are
like . . .

All (*except June*)
*Ci siamo persi! Questa e la
strada?
E lontano? Ciabatta! Aqua!
Miraculo!*

Then . . .

Shhhhhh!

Leah
In the park, by the river, we
find

Gash
a crown of thorns

Leah
somebody's made from . . .
grass . . .

She does . . .

it's very delicate, fragile . . .
this work of art somebody's just
made . . .

Gash
The size of the candles you can
buy!

A gang of muscular men . . . it's
their job all day
to shovel the candle wax that's
dripped
like spunk from

the ginormous candles . . .
they're buttock-deep in candle
wax
I feel a stiffy announcing
itself . . .
religion is so sexy!

Leah
There's nuns priests nursing
sisters
in white with assortment girly
through
to chunky shoes . . .

Joy
There's fucking nowhere to sit
and have a little cognac . . .

June
the seats say '*Malades*'.

Leah
Restrooms say '*Hommes Malades*'
'*Femmes Malades*'

June
We see a man in a wheelchair
coming out of '*Femmes Malades*'.

Gash
Holy God . . . a miracle!

All but June laugh. Then . . .

All
Shhhhhh!

Leah
Hey! June! There's all these
photographs
of people who've been cured!

June
Where?

She scours them avidly . . .

Joy
And they're all about a hundred
fucking
years old, Leah!

Leah
So . . .?

Joy
So nothing *recently* so
Fucking 'Shhh' Yourself.

Gash
'You'll find that you're
in the rotogravure . . .'

Leah
It's an awful, awful place.
People queuing all outfits

June
for the miracle
for the miracle

Leah
They're queuing on
wheelchairs
stretchers
. . . push-along beds!

June
And just look at them!
They are not going to recover!
Their bodies are its disgustingly
obvious
their bodies have had it.

Joy
It doesn't state it anywhere
but nobody else is smoking
fuck it.

She lights a cigarette . . .

Gash
Then the throng

Leah
thickens

Gash
yes!

Leah
like chicken soup

Joy
fucking 'Shh' fucking
Jewish Mother! . . .

Gash
and it's moving up to the hour
for . . .

June
serious serious illnesses start
flocking
wheelchairs beds trolleys
stretchers
there's just . . . this is the place
where you're
really ill you're in the
majority . . .

Joy
Christ!

Gash
    Yes

    St Bernadette   huge
    workload

Joy (*headache*)
    The loudspeakers start
    singing praying

    Some holy singing . . .

Gash
    procession starts
    creeping silently
    and

June
    they just go slowly
    round and round
    wheelchairs
    beds
    those awful awful sick bodies
    round and round.

    Holy music loops . . .

Gash
    Well
    the deal, healing-wise, is . . .
    there's a sacred pool
    not very deep
    and if your sicko's walking
    she wades in
    if she's in a wheelchair
    you push your sicko
    into the middle of it
    wide shallow pool

June
> amazing light

Gash
> and you pray
> you light candles and you pray
> because
> in the holy surround
> in that place of great possibility
> in god's kindness and ability . . .
> Miracles do happen.

> (*Sings.*) 'Fairy tales
> can come true
> it can happen to you . . .
> if you're . . . if you believe . . .'

> We get June a wheelchair
> we push June in . . .
> get a good position . . . central pool
> she sits
> we pray.

> *They all really pray. somehow pray for some time.*
> *The following together and intermixed . . .*

Gash
> 'Hail Mary full of grace
> the Lord is with thee blessed art
> thou among women blessed is
> the fruit of thy womb . . .
> Holy Mary Mother of God
> pray for us sinners now
> and at the hour of our death . . .'

Leah (*transliteration*)
> '*Shem-arr Yis-ra-ale*
> *Adornai elorhaynoo adornai er-*
> *chhad*

Barooch shem Kavord malcootor,
layorlam va-ed . . .'

Joy
>Fuck! (*Then, defiantly . . .*)
>*Om shanti padme ommm*
>*Omm shanti padme ommmm.*
>
>What . . . ????
>
>*Until it is unbearable, then they all stop.*

Gash
>After an hour or so
>we push her out . . .
>
>and
>
>it's incredible
>it's a miracle
>it's happened . . .
>
>there's brand new tyres on
>the wheels of her chair!
>
>*Gash, Leah, Joy all laugh . . .*
>
>No
>that's not what happened
>here's what happened
>nothing
>
>to June.

June
>Not true.
>
>*They all look at her.*

Leah
>She's shagged out.
>Car.

June

    It is a miracle what happens

    but   it's dreadful

    the mist clears from my head

    the scales drop from my eyes

    I can see
    I can see something!

Joy

    Drink.
    A fucking drink!

Leah

    We limp home to Creepy Carl's villa
    And even though there's the
    'No Smoking in the Hire Car'
    rule . . .

    June, Joy and Gash light up . . .

Joy

    There's a place to buy wine . . .
    There . . . there! . . .

Gash

    Leah makes supper.

Leah

    Linguine alla Genovese . . .

Gash

    Apparently it's . . .

Leah

    an old Genoese sailors' favourite!
    just *linguine* tossed with raw
    tomatoes (*American pronunciation.*)

Joy/Gash (*British pronunciation.*)
  tomatoes

Leah
  cilantro . . .

  Brits wait patiently . . .

  Coriander!

Joy
  No meat?

Gash
  And *huge* pieces of . . .

Leah
  raw garlic . . . it's really
  healthy . . . it cleanses your blood.

  Others still smoking and . . .

Joy
  It's fantastic with this . . . what is
  it? . . .
  Côte du . . . fucking French can't
  write . . .

June
  I bet these Genoese seafaring types
  never got colds, hey, Leah?

Gash
  Nor ever scored . . .

June
  We're all up all night with .. . .

  Gash belches.

Gash
  Oh God . . .

Joy belches . . .

Joy
Fuck!

Leah belches . . .

Leah
I'm sorry . . .

June
Enough wind to power a four-masted
Genoese schooner . . .

Synchronised belching . . .

And so
we're sitting at the table in the
garden
and . . .

the light in the picture is
coming from two sources

an external one
the moon

The moon appears.

and one coming
from an internal source . . .

Then . . .

Gash switches on his St Bernadette statue . . .
The lantern lights them, around an outside table

it's really very beautiful

Joy farts.

Gash farts.

Leah

    Now stop . . .
    No cutting the cheese around the
    patio table . . .

    Leah farts.

    They all fart.

All

    Shhhhhhhh!

    This is very funny.

June

    The miracle-workers have somehow all
    agreed
    to drink far too much.

Joy

    This is good this is so good!
    We should take a dozen each
    back . . .

    A night sky, with twinkling stars.

June

    and play in the warm, dark,
    significant garden.

    Drunken bumblers are all out in the garden.

Leah

    So many stars!
    So many, many stars!
    To guide those poor little Genoese
    sailors
    back to . . . Genoesa . . . Genovesia . . .

Gash

    Genoa.

Leah

No, I never even met her!

Oh, this is soo funny. They both laugh.

Gash

St Bernadette's in the
meadow . . . simple dress . . .
Our Lady appears . . . serious frock
Bernadette sings . . .
(*Sings.*) 'It only happens
when I dance with you
that trip to heaven
till the dance is through
with no one else do
the heavens seem quite so near
why does it happen, dear,
only with you?'

A phenomenally drunken Joy stands in the garden.

June

Joy, of course, well out in front
wine-wise . . .

Joy

No.
Oh no!
He's hanging about!
My fucking dead fucking boyfriend's
hanging about!

Gash and Leah dance.

Joy

You weren't invited!

Gash (*sings on*)

'Two cheeks together
can be so divine

but only when those cheeks
are yours and mine
I've danced with dozens of others
the whole night through
but the thrill that comes with spring
when anything could happen
that only happens
with you.'

Leah
Who's leading?
Who's The Girl?
I'm The Girl!
Oh, alright, *you* be The Girl!

As, Joy, dancing with herself . . .

Joy
Don't stand on my feet
Don't   don't!
Don't stand on me!

You're standing on me!

Leah
Joy . . . we're really not!

Joy
Follow . . . follow! You bastard,
we don't even dance well together,
wassat tell you about it all?
Not working not working was it?
If you can't dance with somebody
you shouldn't have sex with them
you know . . .

Gash (*to Leah*)
Well, that's told us.

Leah

Joy.
Pointless question.
Would you like some lovely water?

Joy

I'm going to lie down for a bit.

Under a bush.

Or this vine.

Follows a vine, using it like a handrail.

Don't follow me!

Corporeal beings don't. Joy finds the end of her vine.

Leah

Alright!

Is that dry there?

You'll catch something you won't be
able to get rid of . . .

Shall I fetch your lovely pashmina . . .?

Joy

Why?
Why?
Why?
I'd have talked you out of it
you know I'd have talked you out of
it
is that why you didn't mention it . . .?

Litlle firefly lights appear around Joy.

Now you're here!
Now you're important!

Now you've made an indelible mark!
Now I'll remember you we'll all
remember
you
Mr Sooooo Tragic!
I didn't even love you much . . .
Was that the plan?
Turn that around?
Carve this look on my face?
I can't afford these Lines! . . .
I'm an actress !

Gash sits down with June.

Gash
Well.

June
Well.

Gash
Lourdes!

June
Lourdes!

Gash
How you feeling?

June
Oh. Cured!
You?

Gash
My heart hurts.

June
Mine too.

Gash
You tell me why yours is hurting

Then I'll tell you why mine is
hurting.

Pause. This is very embarrassing.

June

I've been holding a small ball of
faith there
that this ridiculuous crazy stupid
trip might work!

Gash

Faith?

June

Faith.
Meaning Confidence. Reliance.
Trust.
Meaning beliefs in the truth of
religion.
Meaning that which is or should be
believed.
I'd brought hope
into that incense-reeking place . . .
same awful awful hope as   that lot
those poor twigs and sticks and
wigged
. . . losers there . . .

Gash

Listen . . . you're *much* prettier . . .

June

and I looked at them
and my hope
burned off like the mist
earlier this horrible day
with the golden sunlight

and now I can see

64

She touches her breast, her liver . . .

like Jesus in the Caravaggio!!!

I really am
going to die
quite soon.

A long horrible silence. Then: perfect manners . . .

So why is *your* heart hurting?

Gash
Took the dear friend into the grotto
into the very centre of the Holy Pool
into the very epicentre
of where miracles are supposed to
happen . . .

Nothing!

June
No.

Gash
There's no God, is there?

June
Don't think so.

Long pause.

Gash
Christ.

Long pause.

Oh Christ.

June
Well . . . No.
Oh   No.

Gash (*soccer commentary*)
'. . . and St Bernadette has scored an Own
Goal
here on the sacred turf of Lourdes!
he's lost his belief, she's lost her
hope
he's sick as a parrot she's sick as a
parrot.'

It's all such a fucking joke.

Stands up.

Think I'll walk round the village.

Leah
Shall I come?

Gash
It's not a *walk* walk . . .

Leah
Oh.   Oh!
What . . . in a tiny village?
Dans un petit village?

Gash
Peut-être il y'a un cottage.
C'est enfin un cottage dans un
petit village . . .

Leah
Merde! France! Incroyable!

Gash
Ouf! Nous y voila!

Joy
And why fucking *phone* me just before
just
Before your Big Fucking Exit???

It can't have been about your suicide
because it wasn't mentioned!
Was it?
It was just . . .
(*Howie voice.*) 'Joy I'm still
Experiencing *major* depression!'
Hardly Big News!

Communicate with me!!!

It seems he doesn't. She looks for him wildly.

Don't go!
I say when you go!

You're nowhere with me still, you
know . . .
Nowhere!

Leah
Joy . . . do you want a lovely rug
while you're down there?

Joy
Lie down here. Tell me what you see
up there . . .

Leah spreads the rug into the air.

Leah spreads the rug onto the floor.

Gash, cottaging pack assembled . . .

June
Condoms? (*Yes.*)
French phrasebook?

Gash
Dans la tête!

June
Psychic Shield ? (*Yes.*)

Be careful.
Prenez garde.

Gash
Sure.

June
I don't want you getting poorly.

Gash
June . . . I'm going to die
like my father did

June
how was that?

Gash
happily
in his sleep . . .

June
Good.

Gash
Not screaming in terror and
panic . . .
like his passengers . . .

Both smile.

June
Raise your right hand.
Repeat after me . . .
I Gary Gash O'Brien . . .

Gash
I Gary Gash O'Brien

June
Knowing how my friend June loves me

Gash
Knowing how my friend June loves me

June
Do therefore swear a solemn and binding oath

Gash
Do therefore swear a solemn and binding oath

June
To always *obey* June's wishes

Gash
To always *obey* June's wishes

June
Vis-à-vis possibly downright dangerous casual sex

Gash
Vis-à-vis possibly downright dangerous casual sex

June
Life-threatening diseases

Gash
Life-threatening diseases

June
And any nonsense which may end in death

Gash
And any nonsense which may end in death

June
So help me God
So help me God

Gash
So help me Ronda!

He goes out into the dark . . .

June
> *Whoever.* And that night I really thought I'd
> said that for *his* benefit . . .

Joy
> Look!

Leah
> Where?

June
> It was last Easter.
> I'd seen this painting.
> I'd been to Lourdes.
> I was in a garden.
>
> You know, I think Jesus was deeply
> manipulative . . .
> Son of God, right . . .?
> He must have known how everybody
> was going to
> behave . . . disciples . . . soldiers . . .
> friends . . . around that final time in
> the
> beautiful garden . . .

Joy
> there's stars and stars and stars
> and stars
> and stars and stars
> and stars

June
> anyway
> what does he care . . .
> he sitteth on the right hand of God
> all
> 'I'm Immortal Thank You Very Much!'

Leah

Joy, do you want me to take you to
bed?

I meant it in a *purely helpful* way . . .

Joy

Why fucking not?

Joy pulls Leah to her. Kisses Leah.

(*To someone incorporeal.*)
Look. See what I'm doing?
Why fucking not?
Look!

Joy kisses Leah again.

Leah

And I did start to say . . .
'No, Joy, lovely . . . when I said, "Do you
want me
to take you to bed?" I just meant it
in a *purely*
helpful . . .'
but, you know . . . the kiss was really
rather *nice* . . .
and we *were* in France! So . . .

Leah's body changes its mind and goes for it.

June watches them.

June

Of course . . . he had different
friends . . .
Or they cut out the bit where Jesus
gets drunk and quite likes Judas
kissing him . . .
But . . . He must have known
who was going to betray . . .

who was going to stand by
who make the cross . . .
sort out the tomb . . . wash the feet . . .
somebody up there in Divine Light
must have *enlightened* him . . .
so he could run the whole thing . . .
to his entire satisfaction . . .
and
make it a really
memorable and beautiful
Easter . . .

*Leah and Joy take the rug and go to bed. June looks
up at the stars as . . .*

Gash plays and sings a beautiful private song.

Time passes to:

This Easter . . .

Gash (*very sincere*)
It was A Miracle!
June lived!
She Lived!
We get back
wheel her in through the door . . .
there's a pile of letters

riffle riffle
what's this?
A Letter!
Reassuringly Thick Paper, vellum,
embossed . . .

A rip . . . a rustle . . .

'The Bostick-Heinz-Philip Morris
Microcosm Miracle Research
Corporation . . .

Dear June . . .
we think we have finally
discovered a cure
for secondary mammarian cancer
and have chosen you to test our new
miracle cure . . . on account of our
boundless admiration for your
groundbreaking, but flattering
lighting
designs . . .
Please come to our Hospital slash
Laboratory
State-Of-The-Art-Complex
at The Raquel Gimps-Loewenstein
Building,
Miracle Boulevard
New Solutions
New Mexico . . .'

Illness is very expensive.

Her more sporty friends organise a
Charity Cycle Ride on her behalf
along
The Great Wall of China . . .

*Chinese music, as Leah cycles across the stage on a
bicycle.*

It raises
Not quite enough money for the
Air Fare . . .
The Outfits . . .
The Kleenex.

I Step In.

He steps in. Limelight very Garland . . .

I perform my

heart-tugging, tear-jerking
performance piece sensation.
It's St Bernadette reimagined
As a young Garland
Torn between a life in the
Cloistered nunnery
Or a Broadway career.

There's a Lesbian Romance in it.

Joy/Leah
Oh God!

Gash
It's called 'Oyster Parade'.

Joy/Leah
Oh Stop!

Gash
And I perform the last song
To a packed Palladium
Entirely for my friend June.
(*Sings.*)
'If happy little bluebirds fly . . .
beyond the rainbow,
why oh why . . .
can't . . . June . . . ???'

Standing ovation
thunderous applause
more flowers than Kew Gardens
and next day
the reviews
(*Quotes.*) 'Perhaps once in a lifetime a
performer comes along who is
both singer
and saint . . .'

It buys the
plane ticket
she goes
tests pills injections skin
grafts
machines
American knowhow

care

He shows us . . . beautifully . . .

The
anguish
anticipation
tenterhooks . . .
I'm filmed in a Balenciaga black
suit pencil skirt
talking about selfless friendship
I look like Hepburn.

Leah
Katharine?

Gash
Audrey
in

Both
Funny Face . . .!

Gash
Gamine et Jolie-Laide.

The close-ups of me in
the heart-tugging moments
in the bleak hospital corridor . . .
are *all* about *her*

and . . .

she's saved
she's saved
in The Nick Of Time
her Condition's Arrested
The Prognosis Is Reversed!
She's saved!
She's saved!

It's   A Miracle!

He holds it. If only . . .

Just kidding.

We get back.
First Big Surprise is . . .
I surf the internet for
St Bernadette research . . .
Discovered Miss Miracles Died At
Thirty-Five!!!
TB!
And Asthma!
Not a Great Advert!!!
Second Non-Surprise is . . .
We go round to have that red
wine . . .
June
She's not able to drink any . . .
Recovery Hopes are Dashed to The
Ground . . .

Fucking Antibodies are working
their Stealthy
Dark Magic.
Apparently all other cells
the *decent* ones
the ones We *Like!*
Die.

Not *Your Cancers*!
They Have *Immortal* Life!

She's getting
weaker
and weaker
and weaker . . .

June
Don't go into detail
It's really not very interesting . . .
sickness . . . there's no fascinating
history . . .
you just get   less

boring
boring
boring

I spend time thinking . . .
Cancer cells chomping greedily
on me the while . . .
could I have done it differently
better?
exercised? eaten more vegetables?
not gone to parties?
chosen a less susceptible bloodline
to be reincarnated with?
did I hold resentment too often
or nurture anger or bile or
something?
not use all my white corpuscles in
an efficient and military onslaught
against
the mighty C?

Did I miss something crucial
I could have done?

77

Been?

Did I somehow invite this?

Offend   some   God?

Was it my fault?

Note the past tense.

Leah
She's given up.
Gash, I think she's just given
up . . .

June
Why
Why
Why

although I know you don't exist . . .

She looks up . . .

Gods. Why?

She waits, listening for an answer . . . There is none.

The conclusion I arrive at
is

one truth appears to shine ever
bright

Shit Happens.

She lights Gash and Leah . . .

Gash
This man.
Standing on Beachy Head.
Lovely day.
Ground suddenly gives way beneath his
feet.

78

He's falling.
Halfway down, he catches at a branch!
Thank God!
Then . . . the branch starts
tearing away from the tree . . .
He's falling again . . .
Man says,
'Why, God, Why?'
God says,
'I don't know . . .
there's just something about you I
don't like . . .'

June
And one modus operandi for the
Happening Shit

Deal With It.

The rest of the time?
I felt a lot of self-pity
and

I slept.

She sleeps. She looks dead. The others watch her.

Gash (*apologetic*)
Sorry. It's very
undramatic.

Leah is making some jungle creepers . . .

Leah (*whispers*)
I get this nice long job
making props
for this children's show that might
go to the West End
fingers-crossed shit money till
then . . .

Jungle Scenario . . .
monkeys that climb and jump
jungle creepers that grow like
amazingly quickly and . . .

Wrap around things and choke them.

bugs that do a hoedown mid-air mid-show

Does it, miniature . . .

a tree frog that croaks . . .

Does it, big, it's not working . . .

Shit!

She works on it.

I'm really good at making things.
Got the hands.
Got the brain that works
through . . . thinks
gaffer tape brown paper chicken
wire clay
things that link combine mesh . . .

Gash
If God worked in chickenwire
He'd be You.

Leah
I know I can make   things
but can I make this weird odd bizarre
Stunningly Unjewish new thing with
Joy!!!
. . . work?

Crossfades from Leah to Joy.

Joy
Fucking Dead Loss Boyfriend Howie
continued to be dead.

The second year of anybody's death
is like . . .
okay, the joke's over
give me a ring
drop by
run into me in fucking Covent Garden.
Alright, we've had all the Drama
The Funeral the Ash-Scattering . . .
Now, come round let's go out for a
drink
I've so much to tell you . . .
Your funeral for one . . .
You'll never guess who turned up!
That choreographer bitch from Chester
you said you never slept with!
Pinned her in a corner, your dad's
best malt.
Well . . . Who's a liar?
Chester. Derby. And Liverpool!
And after all the fucking whining
about
me and that *Holby City*
lighting cameraman!

Coloured lights here and there tested . . .

But a nano-second after the thought
comes the other thought . . .

oh yes
fuck!
. . . you took that big pile of pills!
Mr Fucking History!

June
Everybody else is so busy
with these bizarre projects and weird
jobs
and perverse relationships . . .

Gash/Leah/Joy
    Hey!

June
    bizarre
    weird
    perverse to someone with no energy
    for them

Others
    Well . . . okay.

June
    I sleep
    I read a bit
    light romances
    anything with a simple forward plot
    and a happy ending

    oh and newspapers
    particularly with weekend glossy
    magazines
    with articles for idiots about
    advances in medicine

    And

    I think.

    She thinks.

Gash (*apologetically*)
    Sorry. It's *very*
    untheatrical.

June
    And
    one day

    I have this bright idea

    A cartoon light bulb lights above her head . . .

It's low and sneaky . . .
It's as low and sneaky as the
Lourdes-Cure Master Plan . . .
Yeah . . . it's a sort of Revenge . . .
(*Thinks.*) Oh. Yes. Delicious.
I pick them off
one at a time . . .
in their hunting seasons . . .

Lights as . . .

Gash
one afternoon
near Christmas . . .
bright clear morning . . .

Christmas lights . . .

Gash (*sings*)
'Jack Frost roasting on an open fire
chestnuts nipping at your nose . . .'

June
Christmas soon.

Gash
Don't.

June
Season of loving and giving.

Gash
Don't.
I'm off loving and giving
Just at the moment . . .
But nobody from The Funding Bodies is loving
Or giving it up for Oyster Parade.
You'd think
religious festival
St Bernadette . . . Garland songs . . .

the fall of religion, the rise of
glamour . . .
God dies!
a Gay perspective . . .
people would put their hands in their
pockets . . .
feel around . . .

June

You would.

Gash

And you'd think one's friends
Would care just one iota
But they're all like
'No, I'm busy'
'No, I'm seeing Joy tonight'
'No, we're going to The Albert
Hall to listen to the *Dalai Lama* . . .'

June

People can be so self-obsessed.

Gash

They can, can't they?

June

Been reading an article . . .
Quite interesting what's happening
in the Netherlands at the moment . . .

Gash

Netherlands. Ding!
This is going to be something
progressive and difficult, isn't it?

June

In this doctor's office . . .
in Amsterdam . . .
there's a teeny-tiny bronze statue of

a young girl . . .
standing on the window . . .
looking out over the canal-riddled
landscape . . .

Gash
The dykes . . . the gays . . . the white
bicycles . . .
are we thinking Christmas, Amsterdam?

June
It's made by
and it's of . . . this girl with bone
cancer . . .

Gash
Oh, here we go . . . heart strings . . .

June
He's been treating her since she was
ten . . .
she knows she's going to die
and he thinks it's medically okay
and humane to provide the drugs
so she can do it

Gash
Do it?

June
Die.
When she choses to do it.

Gash
Call me acute, call me psychic
but . . . I'm sensing a subtext . . .

June
Okay
the disease progresses

she thinks 'If my little legs go, I'll
go.'
Her little legs go. she thinks
'Hey, I can still play guitar . . .
talk to my friends . . .
if I become incontinent, then I'll
go . . .'
Now she's incontinent . . .
but she thinks, 'I'll use nappies
that's okay.'

Gash

The Human Will To Live.
A Magnificent Story Arc! There's a Big
Play in It!

June

Then . . . the doctor does a house call . . .
the little girl
she says 'Something's going in my
brain.
That's enough.
I think I'll die tonight.'
The doctor says, 'I understand.'
There's no need to discuss it.

Gash

Dutch doctor.
So cool!

June

That night, with her parents there
she takes the medicine,
dies.
You okay?

Gash

Yes!

June

Something's going in my brain.
That's enough.
Not fun any more.

Gash

They're always ahead, your Dutch . . .
first to have dykes . . . selling legal
drugs . . . now doctor-assisted suicide . . .

He gets what she is saying . . .

Of course . . . this isn't Amsterdam.

June

No.

Gash

You wouldn't get a doctor to . . .

June

No.
A girl would need help. Even a big
girl.
A really good friend.

Gash

You do remember I'm shallow,
don't you?

June

That's why I thought . . . Gash.
He won't dwell. Afterwards.
And . . . last Easter . . .
in the garden . . .
you did swear a solemn oath.

Gash

In the garden?

Not solemn!

June
> To do what I tell you
> *Vis-à-vis* downright dangerous
> sexual practices
> life-threatening diseases
> and death . . .

Gash
> Because I thought it was to do with
> *Behaviour* at the post-your-funeral party!

June
> The oath was unspecific, but binding . . .

Gash
> Drink was involved.
> I was incapable of . . .

June
> You could still walk to *le petit*
> *village*
> for *le fuck français.*
>
> Still binding.
>
> Please.
>
> *Looks for a long time at Gash.*

Gash
> It's a sin.

June
> But you've lost your faith . . .

Gash
> Damn You Wily Atheists!!!

June
> Promise you'll think about it.

Gash

Promise. I need a blow-job.
British.

Gash goes off as . . .

June

Promise not to tell anyone else!!!

Gash

I promise!

June looks towards Leah . . .

June

Hannukah.

A menorah . . . June lights the candles, one by one as . . . hannukah music.

Heather working on the tree-frog sock puppet. Its croak interrupts their conversation.

Leah

It's like . . . some days . . . she's
lovely . . .
we're like . . . it really works . . .

June

Is she drinking?
(*To us.*) You stop being that interested
in all this . . .
but good manners cost nothing.

Leah

Ah well . . . when she's not, it's
okay . . .
but honestly, it's best when she is
drinking . . .

Tries sock frog. Nothing.

In the Merry phase . . . before Weepy
and . . .
Nasty . . .
You see . . . I think I can make it
work . . .

Tree-frog sock puppet croaks sceptically.

June
But you're not the problem . . .

You need Joy on board
on message
on whatever, Leah . . .

Leah
Yes . . . you're right. Good advice.
She's got to put the work in too . . . be
half of the equation . . . take a certain
amount
of responsibility for a shared
action . . . (*as*)

June (*same time, to us*)
you can autopilot on
all of it
because really   there's nothing
new
you realise
and when you get bored of it
you just play the Most Sick And Needy
Card . . .

June shifts slightly, in pain . . .

Ooogh . . .

Leah
Sorry.
Drivelling On.
Okay?

June (*to us*)
See?
(*To Leah.*) Hey.   I saw this docu-
drama . . .
this woman . . . her mother's dying
of emphysema . . .

Leah
Awful   who was art director?

June
Can't remember. She's going to
naturally die
of suffocation.

Leah
So's this *fucking* tree frog . . .

June
She absolutely dreads this.

Leah
God . . . you would!

June
So the family
negotiate euthanasia
with the family doctor . . .
the doctor comes
they all say their goodbyes
the mother sends them out . . .
because she doesn't want them
actually there when she . . .

Leah
Well you wouldn't . . .

June
They sit outside
after a while the doctor calls them . . .

it's been really quick
she really must have been ready . . .
apparently . . . it was really beautiful
Her Death. And Her Choice.

Leah clocks something.

None of them had any problem
with it at all   after.

June looks at Leah. Leah looks back.

Leah
Oh, June.

June
Please.

Leah
You don't go anywhere, June!
You just stop.

June
I'm ready.

I need a Safe Pair of Hands.

She touches Leah's hand.

Think about it.

Promise you won't say anything . . .

Leah
I promise.

June
Promise you'll think about it.

Leah
I promise.

They both look at Leah's hands.

Tree-frog sock puppet looks from one to the other as Leah's hands fiddle . . . Then it croaks loudly.

June
Nobody wants to do it.

Leah/Gash (*separate spaces*)
I can't do it.

June
Everybody wants to think about it . . .

Leah/Gash
I need to think about this!

June
I need somebody who doesn't think
before they act . . .

Joy

Joy, with a drink, joins June . . .

June
What?

Joy
What happens
the fucker comes in my dreams
and we have sex
it's like he's arriving just to do that
and
I'm turned on
I'm really turned on . . .
even though I know we've finished
and anyway he's fucking dead by his own
hand
and anyway I'm a Buddhist now as you know . . .

June
well . . . ever since you shagged that Shiatsu guy . . .

Joy
ever since that Shiatzu guru
aligned my charkas absolutely so
why's Howie still hanging around?
I mean, shouldn't he be a lotus tree
or a tree frog
or

The sound of a bird . . .

that bird or something by now?

They both listen to the bird.

June
If that's him, he's got more chatty . . .

Joy
But
and
I'm somehow being unfaithful
to Leah . . . which is ludicrous because
I don't embrace the notion of monogamy
as you know!

June
Absolutely   or practise it

Joy
I wake up

I think where is he

then I remember
oh yes
dead

God, I hate fucking Dead People!
June, you have to fucking promise
not to come back and fucking haunt me . . .

June

That's hard . . .

Joy

Well, at least you're going
fucking naturally . . .

June

No . . . it's just . . . I'll be dead . . .

Joy

No self-murder shit involved!

June

and I don't know whether I'll
come back or not . . . see?

Joy

And no fucking me, either!

June

Okay.
I can't remember how to . . . actually . . .
Been so long.

Joy

Because we've *never* fancied one another.

June

No. Our love has always been pure.

Joy

Whatever.
And don't . . . hang around.
Lurking!
Fucking Psychic Stalking!
Making me feel I could have done
something . . .
like Howie . . .

June
I promise.

Joy
Okay.
So what did you want to ask me

and how are you?

June
It doesn't matter.

I'm Fine.

She watches as Gash returns . . .

Gash
I've just been to that garage . . .

Leah
not the one where you had that thing with
the gas-station guy . . .

Gash
Yes.
I still can't go in there
without filling up!
So. How are you?

Stranger.

Lesbian Stranger.

Leah
I'm good.
It's good.

Gash
As good as with Pretty Barry?

Leah says nothing.

Less Blow Jobs, I suppose?

Leah says nothing.

Different Blow Jobs, I suppose?

Leah looks at him.

Moving swiftly on.
This man dies. Goes to Hell.
The devil says, 'We have three rooms
you can choose from.
First room . . . everybody's standing up to
their waists in shit.
Second room . . . everybody's standing up to
their necks in shit.
Third room . . . everybody's standing
knee-deep
in shit, drinking cups of tea.'
Devil says, 'Okay, which do you fancy?'
The man says, 'Well, if it's all the same
to you . . .
I'll take the third room.'
Okay, says the Devil. Man goes in.
The devil says 'Okay. Tea break over.
Back on your heads.'

They laugh.

Gash
I've got this secret I can't tell you.

Leah
Me too.

She asked you. (*Yes.*)

She asked me.

Oh, Gash,

what are we going to do?

97

Gash
The bitch made me promise
to think about it.

Leah
She made *me* promise too!

Both
Let's think Together!!!

They sit somewhere to think . . .

Gash (*to us*)
Undramatic again . . .!
I wish her family were more . . .
she could ask them.

June
No. No!

Gash
Because of course, that would be *Wrong!*

Leah
An *Infanticide Rap.*

Gash
Quite!

Leah
Aged Parents. Prison Time.

Gash
Not a bad *Art Film*. But
No.

Down to us.

They look at June.

Leah
She *is* starting to be in a lot
of . . . (*pain*).

June

The pain really is . . . indescribable . . .

Gash might help Leah with some nice comedy props . . .

Gash

This would be Our Greatest Challenge.

Leah

Absolutely.

Gash

Because we're not *obvious* casting for
Killers.

Leah

Absolutely not obvious.

Gash

Which could work to our advantage . . .
(*Realising suddenly.*) in the
fucking Court Case!!!!

Leah

Worst Case Scenario. What could we get?

Gash

Manslaughter? Aiding and Abetting?
No Death Sentence
fortunately . . .

Both

Phew!!!!

Leah

Unless I'm deported!!!

They contemplate this.

Gash

You do The Crime here . . .

Leah (*phew*)
You do The Time here . . .

Gash
Listen. Let's do what we normally do.

Leah
Okay.   What?

Gash
Let's say, 'Yes, we'll do it.' And hope
something happens so we don't have to do
it.

Leah
Brilliant!

What could happen so we won't
have to do it?

Gash looks at her.

Oh.   Oh.

Gash
Okay!

Tea break over.
Back on our heads.

June
It can't be hard to finish off someone
who's this . . . tired!
Two's enough.
Two's plenty.

Then   shit! . . .
autopilot!
the Leah–Joy Thing!

Joy enters to Leah with bottle and glass . . .

Joy

    Leah Sweetie!
    You have to try this!
    Bison's Grass vodka!!!
    This Polish director I did that
    Demon-possessed nun cameo for in Prague
    Brought it back for me.
    You have to toss it down in one big gulp!

    She makes her . . .

    How good is that?

    What's up?

Leah

    I've got a secret I can't tell you.

Joy

    Aw. Sweetie. Have another . . .

    Makes her as . . .

June

    The you-can-never-tell-one-half-of-
    couple-anything-you-don't-want-the-other-
    half-to-know-unless-you've-
    Stipulated-the-promise-is-*exclusive* Thing!

Joy

    What?
    What?
    What???
    She is so fucking selfish!

Leah

    She doesn't want *you* to . . .
    She wants me and Gash to . . .
    Oh, honestly . . . this is so typically June!
    If she didn't want me to tell you she
    could have said the Promise is *Exclusive*!

June
    Shit!
    Brain!

Joy
    Why doesn't she want me to . . . ?

Leah (*straight face*)
    Because she knows you're
    a Buddhist and life for you is sacred,
    Joy . . .

Joy
    Oh shut up!
    Why not Me?
    Oh, right . . .!
    Implicated in the Howie suicide mess
    so police are going to be . . . hey, Prime
    Suspect!
    Send Helen Mirren round . . .
    (*Helen Mirren.*) 'I'm Detective-Inspector Jane Tennison
    something stinks here and I think it's
    you,
    Suicide Mary!'

Leah
    No! No! No!
    It's because she knows how . . . Howie . . .
    how you . . . how it's always in your . . .
    how it hurts you . . .

Joy
    That fucking creep? Hurt me!!!

    Why can't people just . . .
    die naturally these days?
    Of Old Age!
    Who the fuck does she think she is?
    Fucking God?

You're not doing it!
It's fucking criminal, Leah!
She can't expect you to . . .

'No!' Leah

Leah

Leah!

No.

You're not doing it.

Leah (*pause*)
Yes. I am.
me and Gash . . .
promised

Joy
This isn't House on The Fucking
Prairie!!!
You're not Little Fucking . . . that
blonde kid!!!
You don't have to keep fucking promises

Leah
You do. Actually . . . sometimes . . . you do.

Pause.

I do.

Oh God. I *am* going to do it!!!

Joy
Ah.

Fine then.
Stick with Gash.
I think I'll have a drink.

Leah
>Fine then.
>Stick with Howie.
>I think I won't have a drink.

>*Joy leaving . . .*

Joy
>I think you won't have a shag either!

Leah
>I think you won't have one either!

Joy
>Don't count on it!

Leah
>Try and make it with someone
>who's alive then!

>Die!

>That's what you want, isn't it?

>Smoking??? Drinking to Oblivion???

>*Joy has gone.*

June
>You were very dramatic, Leah!

Leah
>I know!

>*Much more dramatic than previously*:

>'Stick with Howie!'

>'Die!'

>'That's what you want, isn't it?'

June
>Very good!

Leah

Well out of it.
Well out of it!
Phew! What?

She bursts into tears, then stops efficiently and completely.

And it is For the Best.
(*To us.*) Because
things really start to accelerate . . .
the line on the chart
starts . . . (*descending*)
June's in hospital
she's out of hospital
it's
things are quite
it's getting time . . .

Gash

They start giving her a lot a lot of
medication

June

I write out this living will thing
to try and keep them both in the clear

Gash

We get these seminars in Friend
Murder from June . . .

Leah, Gash attending . . .

June

. . . if the medication doesn't
seem strong
enough . . .
if all else fails . . .
in my bedside drawer . . .

Leah looks, takes out a plastic bag, holds it while she looks, looks in the plastic bag . . .

Leah

There's nothing in here . . .
there's . . . (*Suddenly, she gets it . . .*)
Oh June.

June

You have to do the plastic-bag-
over-my-face thing . . .
Make Sure.

Horrible pause. Then:

Gash

But not this one . . .

June

Why?

Gash shows her. The bag says 'Sainsburys. Organic. A bag for life.'

The three of them laugh and laugh and laugh.

No. Not that one.
A plain one.

Gash

Prada, or Dolce and Gabbana /
. . . or Gucci . . . ?

June

A plain one.

Gash

I'm going to kill my friend.
Without a Good Label.

Leah

And   no Joy.

Joy with drink, smoking . . .

Joy
I love drinking!
I love smoking!
I love Getting Out Of It!
Getting Out Of It.

She thinks

That's Dying . . . isn't it?

She thinks.

Fuck!

I want to die?

Sits down to think this through . . .

June
I rethink this whole miracle thing
I used to . . .
see men in armour a white horse
details of flowers a flash of
Venetian red
bees making honey   a lion.
A bed being let down through a roof.
Sun   on a sword   strong sinewed forearms
a horn held aloft the mouth
blowing . . .
gold leaf over a blue veil . . .
when
actually
a miracle is
mayonnaise
Post-It notes
a baby
toast
if you're a Jackson Pollock fan
splatters.

There is a light. June does not make it.

Ah.

And

Light.

Gash (*telling June*)
This man goes to a doctor,
says, 'Doctor, doctor, I keep thinking I'm a
moth.'
The doctor says, 'You need a psychiatrist.
I'm a paediatrician . . . why did you come to
me . . .?'
The man says, 'Oh, I just saw your light
and
I was drawn to it . . .'

June
This long white tunnel
and in the walls of it . . .
dead people I know

*She reaches out to almost touch something in the
direction of . . .*

Grandma?

Graham!

Howie . . .?

The big miracle of Lourdes
for me
was
I was released from having to live
and
once you do devote yourself to the
business of dying
that's a fascinating project too!

Joy, big bottle of mineral water, a potted small tree,
a dog-eared photograph.

She is both drinking the water and watering the plant.

Joy
Come here.

She pulls photograph to her . . .

This is the first conversation we've had
sober.
Me sober.
So.
(*Enormous shout.*) You killed yourself,
you bastard!
(*Same enormous shout.*) And now, fucking
June!
So I'm not going to see her at the moment
because I might just fucking kill her
out of sheer irritation!

She bursts into tears.

I need a drink!

You must have really wanted out, huh?

I do understand, actually. I do.

But.

Dying's not just about You!

What do you think about this thing with
Leah, then?

Leah!!!

She's actually very nice!
She's actually very . . . lovely actually . . .!
Kind of different kind of thing for me . . .
I mean not . . . frantic like . . . (*you and me*).

But it's over, so fuck her!

I don't like any of this, Howie!

Don't you think I deserve a drink?

A cigarette?

I need to go out!

I need to see . . .

Fuck!!!!!

She goes over to June . . . with the potted tree . . .

I'm still fucking mad at you so
don't think this is a Forgiveness Thing
or a Helping-You-To-Top-Yourself Thing
I'm only here because you're a
distraction from . . .

She stops, looks at June who is looking at something . . .

The *Big* News is
I come in . . .
she's staring at something in terror
her hands gripped to the . . .

June
Oh!
Oh!
Oh!

Joy
Nurses on the shift too few too
harassed to notice
I hold her hand

June (*crying*)
Oh.
Oh.
Oh . . .

Joy
I complain
'She's fucking terrified here!'
Nursey-Wursey's all
'Mmm . . . I think that dosage needs
adjusting . . .'

Leah
This means turning it down so
low that she . . .

June (*screaming in pain*)
Oh!
Oh!
Oh!

Joy
The nurse is like, (*Like nurse.*) 'No, no,
your friend is not receiving
inadequate care . . .
This is how we have to do it.
Sorry.'

Gash
The choices.
Drug-induced dementia.
Or unbearable pain.

Joy
Or fucking murder.

Long pause. They look at one another. A decision is reached.

Leah
All our respective religions
give this a Big No-no.
We have a problem.

Joy

Yes.

But so has June.

She's not dying like this!

June

And on Good Friday.

Joy

Last Easter

Gash

we set about stopping it.

Joy

We bring her home.

They pick her up. Stage lift.

June

I was glad I'd talked to them . . .

because . . .

I hadn't counted on . . .

hadn't really understood I'd go . . .

(*Huge shout.*) crazy with pain!!!!!

Arches hugely in their arms. They set her down somewhere.

Leah

We have to totally guess the dose

that will kill her.

Joy

This nurse who helps settle her in is all

very *ER*, very Nurse Abby Lockhart,

'She's not allowed more than a

certain level because any more

will be lethal . . .'

Leah

So Joy's all Oscar-nomination . . .

Joy (*acting*)

No no I understand . . .
I completely understand . . .
so
so how much is that . . .
exactly . . .
that level of drugs
that is
you know
this side of   gulp . . . lethal?

Leah

And the nurse is like

Gash

Nurse Ratchet.

Leah

One Flew Over the . . .

Gash

'0.357 milligrammes would put her
in the danger area . . .'

Leah

so we take that figure . . .

Joy

and fucking double it

Leah

Better Safe Than Sorry.

Joy

Easter weekend.
Good Time. Holiday.
Skeleton Service. Sorry!

Leah

We make her flat nice.
Jungly.
It's what I had!

Gash

Anyway
she stops ricocheting with pain
she stops moaning
that look on her face . . .

He does it . . . a rictus of agony . . .

is
ironed smooth . . .

He starts singing to her, softly . . .

'Never saw you look
quite so pretty before,
never saw you dress
quite so handsome what's more . . .
I could hardly wait
to keep our date
this lovely Easter morning
and my heart beat fast
when you came through the door . . .'

Leah erects a jungle of strangling creepers . . .

Leah

I give her last few days a
jungle creeper
something
nature
animal kingdom
Survival Special kind of feel
I mean
Death is its Nature isn't it?

June (*eyes closed, REM, very quietly, watching an internal film*)
Snake eats a rat
maggots pick clean a mouse
a crocodile rears out of the river
brings down a zebra . . .

Joy
Of course
it's possible we just
send her hurtling into
a terrible terrifying unknown landscape.

June (*too quiet for them to hear*)
You didn't.
Really you didn't.

Leah
We don't know

Joy
because the fucking nurses
a) don't fucking know
and
b) don't fucking help . . .

Gash
It takes her most of the Easter weekend
to die
from the moment
we set about killing her

All Three
We have to press the button.

Gash
On this   like a hideous piece
of costume jewellery . . .
clipped to her   dying outfit!

They do it together . . .

Leah
that pumps the morphine cocktail
into her

Joy
Think about it
ending on a cocktail
very Scott Fitzgerald
very Noël Coward.

They all sit round her, one by one.

Leah
Then . . . it's sort of sitting Shiva
. . . a tad early

Gash arrives last, with plastic bag.

Gash
Just in case . . .

Leah
she slips

Joy
assisted, ladies and gentlemen
of the jury

All Three
by these hands

They put them up, surrender.

Leah
into a final sleep

June
from which I never wake

Leah
I hope it was painless

I think it was painless

Joy
we just don't know

Gash
we think she just . . .
slipped away . . .
(*Sings.*) 'In your Easter bonnet
with all the frills upon it
you'll be the finest fellow
at the Easter Parade . . .'

Etc . . . Into big soundtrack end of 'Easter Parade'.

Joy
It's fucking *ER*
or *CSI* or
fucking Initials TV . . .
nurse who comes in
after she's pronounced dead
after they take her away
to take
away the *Medical Morphine Jewellery*
and shit is like . . .
'There's actually a puzzling amount
of her drug allowance that I am
unable to track down . . .'
I'm like, 'Oh?'
and she's like, 'This is serious.
The police should be called.'
We're in the fucking *NYPD Blues* now!
I say, 'Well, Nurse, I'm going to
leave that one with You.'
I'm all ready for *Bad Girls*, *Prisoner
Cell Block H*.
Handcuffs.
Whatever.

Gash (*putting half-eaten sandwich in the plastic bag*)
I corrupt the circumstantial evidence
at the crime scene.
I can't tell you how relieved I am
we didn't need this.
. . . if you think she looked awful
in the wig . . .
picture her in this!
Police come.
Cordon off the house.

Leah
No they didn't.

Gash
Okay. They just come.

Joy
Very Reality TV.
They're all . . .
(*Northern accent.*) 'Sarge, I dunno
if it's an offence for t' mates to be around
while sumbdy's
committing suicide . . .'

Leah
Talk to us . . .
I just . . . collapse
and cry
and two officers
one asking and the other just . . .
crying . . .

Joy
The old 'Good-Cop-Wet-Cop' Routine.

Gash
Then the police grab hold of us . . .
smash us against the wall

Joy
take out their truncheons
they hit us
all in body areas that
won't show bruising,
saying, 'You killed this innocent woman.
You earned her trust
then you murdered that
sweet hairless thing.'

Pause.

Gash
Just kidding . . .

Leah
It would have made a much better story . . .

Gash
But actually, the nurse goes . . .

Joy
'Well . . . perhaps someone
got the numbers wrong . . .'

and I say, 'You sound like my accountant.'

Gash
And the police . . .

Joy
They pretend it never happens either.

And that was that.

Gash
Drama-wise . . . Big anti-climax.

June
And
one extraordinary thing . . .
at the very end . . .

I start bloody believing in something
my mind comes to no conclusion
but my body does
it ends

Leah
suddenly
this   change

Gash
Cliché Alert.

Leah
She's peaceful

Joy
Her face!

June
Peace

Joy
oh God! her hands

June
and
there's absolutely   no reason

I'm completely happy

Joy
like she's looking at

Gash (*very apologetic*)
Cliché Alert!

June
the most beautiful light

A beautiful light streams.

I can't tell you how I felt
I can't tell you what I saw

I'm dead.

Lights out on her.

She disappears.

Gash (*a big shout to the highest point of everything*)
Is there anything there?

Is it Heaven?

Is God there?

If anything is there, it gives no sign.

Pause.

Joy
And she rose again from the dead
as

Art!

Leah
Here's what happens

I miss her

I miss her

I miss her

but my work's excellent!

I mean, Caravaggio????
Eat your heart out!

Produces the tree frog, which croaks and moves perfectly.

Gash
The bitch!

Joy
Well, she just joins the
rest of the fucking crew

up there
down there
over
beyond
wherever
whatever!

Leah

And she really ruins our next Easter
Remembering her!

Gash

She becomes
in our stories
wittier
better
more dramatic
younger
more   spiritual
we of course are just human

if I could paint she'd be some sort of
influence

Joy

I've used her once or twice
mainly in like tart's parts
single mothers
for telly actually
and my unresolved anger
over her early death
is *perfect* for Lady Anne!

and, Fair Do's, she never haunts me . . .

Gash

And when I need to cry . . .
as . . . Bernadette . . . as Judy . . .
I recall . . . when her hair dropped out

the wig
when she said
'When it's not fun any more,'
when she . . .

He's crying.

Oh, Mary Lou . . . ise!

He goes outside . . . Leah runs to watch . . .

Leah
He's after a quick shag.

Joy
Who isn't?

Leah
Me.

Joy
You see . . . there's the problem.
Leah. Us. Noooooo.
It was Drink.
It was *La Belle France*.
It was fucking Lourdes!
It was Grief.

Leah
It was Hope.

Joy
We'll never make this work.
It would take a miracle.
People die.
There's no such thing as miracles.

Leah
Well, you know,
I think there are actually.
But they need a hell
of a lot of chicken-wire.

Gash returns . . .

Gash
There's nobody out there.

Joy
There's stars and stars and stars
and stars.

Leah
That's enough stars, Joy . . .

Gash
Tell me something nice.

Leah
The summit of Everest
is made of marine floor.

It is amazing . . .

Gash
Something else.

Leah
If a person on Betelgeuse was
looking through a telescope powerful
enough to see Earth . . . now
they'd see dinosaurs walking around
here.

Joy
That's fucking amazing . . .

It is amazing.

Gash
Something else.

Leah
No. Your turn.

Gash
Something nice.

Joy
Something amazing.

Gash
Well
Gandhi
the great spiritual leader of India
most of the time
he walked barefoot
which, of course, made his feet
badly callused.
And because he fasted . . .
he was very frail
and also
he had really bad breath . . .

Gash
So
he was a super-callused fragile mystic
plagued with halitosis . . .

Joy and Leah laugh.

Leah
Lovely.

Joy
One more.
Just fucking one.

Gash
This woman
she's dyslexic
she's agnostic
she's insomniac

she stays up all night

wondering if there
is a dog . . .

They smile.

Stars come out fade to black.

The End.